Help Me Understand My Child

Help Me Understand My Child

A MOTHER'S TRUTH ABOUT AUTISM

Florence Bracy

Bugle Horn Press

Help Me Understand My Child
A Mother's Truth About Autism

ISBN-13:9780692956168
ISBN-10:0692956166
Library of Congress Control Number: 2017956481

Cover Design by Jeff Fontelera
Artwork: by Musikavanhu

Bugle Horn Press
Los Angeles, California
www.buglehornpress.com

To my beloved son, Brad.

Without you, there would not be me in this work.

Love you,

Mom

Table of Contents

Foreword

HEREIN YOU WILL FIND A concise and detailed journey of advocacy. This book reveals the commitment, perseverance, and positive outcome that a mother experienced in advocating for her son with special needs, specifically autism. In it, Ms. Bracy has captured the steps that need to be taken by anyone who is the caretaker or care provider of a challenged individual. She gives readers the day-by-day, step-by-step actions that must be taken to receive necessary services and treatments for a special needs child.

Three things are explored in this testimonial that anyone who is concerned about seeing that the proper opportunities and services are provided:

- Do not allow any stigmas or undue bureaucracy to stop you in your quest for assistance.
- Be forthright and persistent in your request for assistance.
- At no time should the words *no* or *never* stop you from pursuing whatever area of need must be met.

Ms. Bracy has well illustrated what it is to be a true champion of advocacy. This book is a must-read for those who are charged with the proper care of a special needs individual.

Bravo, Florence! You have done a great job!

Ralph Dawson
RD Counseling, Inc.
(Former Chair of the Counseling Department,
California State University, Los Angeles)

Acknowledgments

I have many people to thank, but first I would like to thank God for giving us our son, Brad, who has taught us many lessons. I also thank my loving husband, Charles, whose support and commitment to work together as a team has been instrumental in Brad's success. To my daughter, Brittany, who loves her brother like a second mother, I thank you for being you. Thanks also go out to my relatives, friends, and colleagues for your support and understanding over the years.

There are several other incredible individuals I would like to thank—especially Ms. Dianne Lewis and Ms. Elissa Henkin. Without their passion and expertise in the field of special needs, specifically the needs of children with autism, our family would not have gained access to or received the vital services and resources to which Brad was entitled.

Two of Brad's biggest cheerleaders were his one-on-one-assistants, Ms. Deborah Lindsey and Ms. Parkhideh Tangestani, also known as "Ms. Perry." With unwavering faith, persistence, and commitment, they were greatly supportive in helping Brad progress through middle school and high school.

I was given two pieces of advice that quickly became my driving force and motivation. The first was from clinical psychologist Dr. B. J. Freeman. Referring to autism, she told me, "Don't be afraid of the label. It will open doors for you." Back then I couldn't see how, but years later I see that she was right.

Dr. William Takeshita, who was our son's optometrist, gave me the second great motivator. He said, "It's kids like Brad who deserve a chance."

My thanks to both those doctors for their words, which fueled me spiritually to keep going against all odds, no matter what.

The opinions and feedback of numerous people went into writing this book: family members, friends, parents of children with special needs, coworkers, and educators. Among the many who helped along the way, I would particularly like to acknowledge Sheiron Barasa, Roxanne Williams, Sonya Spears, Cecelia Lumpkin, Adele Bayless, Lorraine Hooper, Anita Miller, Ernie Frazier, Alretha Thomas, Darin Early, and Ralph Dawson.

My editors are the backbone of my story as presented here: Ms. Martell Randolph-Rutter, who helped me develop the story and recall some situations I had forgotten and others I did not think were important. Ms. Deanna Brady, my substantive, content, and line editor, who improved my manuscript by correcting the grammar and punctuation. She heard my voice maintained it, and added her gift of wordsmithing while revising and polishing the text. I am indebted to both of these ladies.

All of you have helped to make this book possible, and I will forever be grateful.

Finally, I would like to thank the Los Angeles Unified School District (LAUSD) because, despite some bureaucratic reluctance and resistance, my son benefited immensely from the long-fought-for and hard-won services he received.

Introduction

Before embarking on my journey into the world of accessing special needs services for my son, Brad, the word *tolerance* had never resonated much with me. My goal from day one was to mainstream Brad into "typical" activities for his age. A byproduct of pursuing this goal was that I learned the idea of tolerance, a concept that would very quickly become an invaluable guiding principle along the way.

In the past twenty years, *autism* has been the fastest growing diagnosed developmental disorder. Experienced by both children and adults, it is characterized by social, communicative, neurological, and behavioral challenges. Each case displays unique traits and features, and the severity of the disability varies from case to case.

When you have a child who you think is normal, and then you learn that he or she is not, this is a very traumatic event. On some level it's a tremendous blow to your ego, and therein begins a very long walk through the slow-moving process of grieving, in which you find yourself longing for the child you dreamed of having.

Parents of a child with autism may, at some future point, find themselves on the other side of that long process of grieving with a deep commitment to loving the child they have and supporting that child's right to a full and gratifying life. This book captures some of the deep feelings I experienced on that journey.

From the moment of our son's formal diagnosis of autism at eight years old, my husband, Charles, and I have made it our mission to provide him with not only a "normal" life but also the best life we can possibly give him. Writing and keeping a journal of my experiences for twelve years while raising my son has been both cathartic and immensely enriching. It has helped me to recount the steps of the passage that has led me to the place where I am today.

Each step of the journey has been part of a humbling odyssey. If you can imagine (or know what it's like) being sent almost endlessly from one person, agency, doctor, or school to another to try to find real answers, then you have some idea of what we were up against. When you factor in the additional tasks that are sometimes necessary to obtain those answers—such as asking for help, writing letters, employing advocates, and obtaining or approving additional testing—a clearer picture of the challenges we faced begins to emerge.

I am sharing my reflections and insights on the pages that follow in order to help other families, professionals, and community members to understand this rapidly growing disorder. I hope to inspire and help guide anyone in need of accessing resources and services for special needs individuals.

One of the most important lessons I've learned in my role as an advocate is that half the battle in getting the right answers lies in asking the right questions. As a mother and as an advocate attempting to navigate my way around a convoluted system to get the services Brad needed, I learned that I needed a little patience and a lot of persistence. At times, it was all very complex, but nevertheless it was possible to accomplish.

I firmly believe that as parents, professionals, and community members, it is our duty to advocate for those with special needs. We can be their tireless advocates on the front lines and their first lines of defense, applying our voices and instilling our strength. In supporting our children with special needs, we learn that there are no distances too great to travel and no barriers too big to be broken down. When we are teaching tolerance to others along the way, which imparts respect for individuals with special needs, we make society a better place for all of us.

Author's Note: This is a true account of my story. Some of the names are authentic, but most have been changed to protect the privacy of those involved.

One afternoon I was talking to my daughter Brittany, who is a teacher. She had just finished reading what I had written in my journal, which I was thinking of making the foundation of a book.

She asked, "But, Mom, how did you *feel?* Readers want to know how you *feel!*"

"Okay," I told her. "Here's how I feel. Being a parent of a child with special needs is bittersweet."

I have often found myself repeating this mantra: "Just let me feel *normal.*"

Kindergarten: We're Only Just Beginning

As was typical of a working mom on a Tuesday morning, I was on autopilot, and hurrying to get out of the house. I had been rushing Brad my five-year-old son, trying to make it on time to Kern Academy, a small, private elementary school where he attended.

I got in the car preoccupied with driving and thinking about my duties at work and my to-do list for home. I wasn't especially attuned to Brad's demeanor that day, at least not any more than usual.

When we got to the academy I drove up the school's driveway the same way I had every other morning, expecting my son to grab his lunch and backpack and jump out of the car obediently, as always.

But this morning was different. My son unbuckled his seatbelt, climbed onto the backseat window shelf, and curled his body into a fetal position.

He said, "The teacher is mean, I'm scared, and I don't want to go to school."

It was very unlike him to behave this way. I didn't quite understand what he meant, but I couldn't get much more out of him.

I coaxed him down from the window and escorted him into the classroom. Once inside I told the staff that he had not wanted to come to school that morning, and I repeated what he'd said about the teacher being mean.

After about a week of the same unusual behavior from him, I decided to meet with the principal, Ms. Jackson, with whom I shared a good relationship. Principal Jackson assured me that my son's teacher, Mr. Baron, was a good teacher and that she thought perhaps the problem was with my son, but I was not satisfied with her response on the matter.

After another week of Brad's continued uncharacteristic behavior, I decided to meet with the principal again, only this time with my husband, Charles, by my side. Principal Jackson remained confident in the teacher's conduct and did her best to reassure us that there was no problem.

I had been an active parent at the academy for the previous six years, from the time our daughter had first attended the school. I couldn't help but feel a sense of betrayal that the principal had so easily dismissed my son's reaction to the teacher. I was definitely not pleased with the fact that my concerns were not being addressed. I decided then and there that it was time to sever our relationship with the school.

The new plan was to send Brad to our local parish school, Ansal Lutheran. A fellow church member whom I knew well, Ms. Calley, was the kindergarten teacher at the school.

Brad loved it there. They had lots of playtime at the new school, which was very different from Kern Academy, where they focused primarily on academics.

After two months, Ms. Calley shared with me that she had observed that Brad played *parallel* to the other children and not *with* them. I wasn't alarmed by her observations and didn't read too much into them at the time. I simply explained to her that he was a loner and liked to play by himself.

I later learned that Brad not being able to articulate to me how his teacher was "mean" was actually a language-delay problem for a five-year-old child. Playing parallel with other children his age instead of playing with them directly was actually a characteristic of autism, but at that point I didn't know yet, what to attribute Brad's behavior.

First Grade

Public school became an option for my son when we were looking for some relief from the costly private-school tuition. We decided to move Brad to our neighborhood school, which was five miles away.

Because of low enrollment in certain areas, buses were provided, and most of the children from our neighborhood rode the school bus to Cullen Elementary. This was a 45-minute bus ride each way. I was uncomfortable with Brad taking the bus, so I took him to school and also paid for the after-school program, which ran from 3:00 to 6:00, and I picked him up from there at the end of the day.

The fall semester had only been in session for about three weeks when I went to pick Brad up from the after-school program, and Carol, the program coordinator said, "I haven't seen Brad. He wasn't dropped off by his teacher today."

I stood there stunned and speechless. After class dismissal each day, the classroom teacher was responsible for bringing the children to the after-school program, also conducted on the campus. What did Carol mean, she had not seen him?

I mentally reviewed that morning's routine, reassuring myself that I had seen Brad get in line with his class before I drove away from our drop-off point. Not recalling anything out of the ordinary, I went straight to the principal's office to call the school district's bus yard to see if Brad might have gotten on the bus accidentally, had been left on the bus, or had gotten off at some random bus stop. Then Carol and I began to retrace his path.

The bus route included several stops before the last one, which was at William Hills Elementary, near our house. After an hour of making frantic phone calls and driving around, we found Brad sitting on the steps at William Hills Elementary. He had gotten on the bus and gotten off at the William Hills stop. There was no adult supervision on the campus anywhere. We estimated that he had been sitting by himself on the front steps of the school for three hours.

When he saw me approaching he said, "Mom, where were you? I was waiting for you. What took you so long?"

I hugged him and cried with relief and joy, but I was livid that the Los Angeles Unified School District had failed me. I had left my precious child in their care, and he had been left alone on the school steps unattended. He could have been hurt or kidnapped!

It was around this time that I learned that there were other parents who were also concerned about safety issues and that this was a problem for more than just me. I wrote a letter to the LAUSD, outlining our concerns regarding the lack of supervision on the school grounds during after-school hours, and it was submitted with twenty-five parent signatures.

That letter I wrote to LAUSD was the first of many letters of concern. Years later, I learned that LAUSD did eventually assign supervision on the school grounds during after-school hours, which now protects all the children. I felt victorious and was pleased to know that my efforts had not been in vain.

The actions of just one person can start a whole chain of events that benefit many.

Second Grade: Signs Up Ahead

The following school year, the school district approved a policy that allowed the children in our neighborhood to attend the closest elementary school to their home. For us that was William Hills Elementary. I enrolled my seven-year-old in school for the semester, and Brad was excited about walking to school, just as I had done as a child his age.

Things went well throughout the year. Three weeks before the end of the term I was invited to a Student Study Team, (SST) meeting. An SST is a group of teachers, administrators, and psychologists who are concerned with student academics and/or behavior issues. Parents are invited to attend these meetings and are considered a part of the team.

During the SST meeting, the school staff expressed their concern about Brad's lack of interaction with the other children.

I assured them, "If there was organized play during recess and lunchtime, I'm certain that he would play with the other children."

The librarian had told me that Brad often found refuge in the library during lunch and recess and that he was a good helper there. I had also noticed for myself that when I picked him up after school I would sometimes see him strumming his fingers along the chain-link fence surrounding the schoolyard, not playing with anyone else. (I later learned that this was a type of behavior known as *stimming,* which children with autism often utilize to calm themselves.)

After hearing the SST group's concerns, I took matters into my own hands. I wanted to make sure Brad was on task academically, so I sat in the classroom with him several times. I observed that he read better than most of the students in his class, and he was doing well in math.

I was satisfied with his academic performance, but I was still concerned about his loner status.

That SST meeting took place in June of 1999, and that was the first time I suspected that there might be a problem, but I did not know what it was or where to get help.

Third Grade: A Step in the Right Direction

A NEW CHARTER SCHOOL WAS opening in the community, and I decided to enroll Brad in it for the next school year. It was modeled after some of the independent schools that included an accelerated curriculum.

All was going well until December of 1999. Brad was receiving school work that included more critical-thinking assignments, such as learning how to tell time and writing stories, but over time I could see that he was gradually losing ground.

Dealing with it in my own way, I purchased additional educational supplements from a teacher-supply store. I bought such teaching aids as *Hooked on Phonics*, at the time a well-respected reading program, and workbooks to practice with him at home.

As I tried to help Brad with his homework, frustration crept in. When working with him on his reading, I noticed that he was having difficulty in comprehending and sequencing and was unable to remember the details of the story just after he had read it. I would have him draw pictures to assist him to recall the details of the story, but he could not tell me what he had just read. I was soon at my wits' ends and needed some help.

In March of 2000, the school administrators called another SST meeting. Charles and I met the teacher, psychiatric social worker, and several administrators who were in attendance. They were all stumped.

Brad was very fond of *The Iron Giant*, an animated feature film that was popular at the time. Not only could he draw the cartoon figure, but—even more impressive—he was able to build a seven-foot replica of the main character using just cardboard pieces, scrap paper, and tape.

Brad was reading above his grade level but could not answer any of the review questions at the end of the story. He knew all of the math facts of addition, subtraction, multiplication, simple division, and even square roots, but he could not do multiple-step math problems. He seemed to excel in so many areas, but in others, I was still mystified as to the root of the problems.

Despite Brad's academic skills and my efforts to assist him in his critical thinking assignments, at the end of the day, you have to know when to call for more backup or send for additional troops!

Language Alert

EVERY SUMMER WE ENROLLED BRAD in a course of swimming lessons. The summer of his eighth year, we decided to let him take lessons with a small group of kids from the neighborhood.

Mr. Garner, a tall, robust, and athletic man in his fifties, provided private and semiprivate lessons to students at his beautiful home. We had been there three times, and Brad had enjoyed the lessons. Mr. Garner threw toy rockets into the deep end of the pool, and all the students would swim and dive to retrieve them. Brad enjoyed himself and felt a sense of accomplishment when he brought back the rockets.

During the third session, Mr. Garner repeated the drill with the rockets, and Brad swam to the bottom of the pool. Suddenly, he came up from underwater crying and yelling, "I'm scared, I'm scared!"

I didn't know what had happened, so after a few minutes I told the instructor to let Brad get out of the pool. I consoled him and finally figured out that he wasn't able to hold his breath long enough that time, but he couldn't explain specifically what had happened.

This incident made me realize later that even though Brad could speak, he did in fact have a severe language processing problem that could put him in danger in the future if people weren't able to understand what he meant.

We must listen carefully to our children. They are always telling us things, even though they may not have the words to express themselves.

The "A" Word

At the SST meeting, the psychiatric social worker had reported having observed Brad exhibiting—verbal outbursts, chewing on pencils, throwing tantrums, and displaying stubbornness—but I hadn't seen this type of disruptive behavior for myself. Afterwards, Charles and I had agreed to meet with her again at a later date.

We had a follow-up meeting with her two weeks later and were asked to complete some medical history forms for Brad. At the end of our meeting she suggested that Brad might have autism.

I was shocked. Immediately, I imagined what I thought was a typical autistic child, sitting in the corner of a room and hitting their head against the wall. I insisted, "You have to be out of your mind!"

Before Brad entered the third grade, my daughter, Brittany, who is eight years older than her brother, volunteered at the summer camp he'd attended. The counselor there, a college student, asked my daughter, "Does Brad have autism?" When she told me what the counselor asked, I said, "That guy is a jerk and just some young kid who doesn't know anything!"

That was the first time anyone had used the "A" word in describing Brad, and now this psychiatric social worker was suggesting the same diagnosis.

I was advised to go to UCLA Medical Center in order to get the most comprehensive psychological testing for the condition. In June of 2000 I spoke with our health insurance company and learned that they would pick up 100% of the costs at UCLA. I quickly tried to make arrangements to have Brad tested and finally got an appointment for the assessment three months later, in September.

Acceptance isn't always easy, but often it is the first step to finding solutions.

Third Grade Again: Learning to Trust

I REALIZED THAT BRAD WAS not progressing in his third grade class and was in danger of possibly being held back. Contemplating another change of schools, I pondered whether I should whisk him away to somewhere else and try to remain anonymous, or stick it out at the current one and endure the students calling him names and teasing him because he had failed.

Running away to another school, as I had always done with him before, really wasn't an option, because we had been to all the other public schools in the area and had left them all for various reasons. We really couldn't afford a private school, so I decided to stay and not to protest the inevitable decision to have him repeat the third grade.

When fall came, I dreaded having to explain to any of Brad's classmates' parents why he was not in their child's class anymore. I shared my dilemma with my great aunt, who said, "He needs to learn that he has to fulfill the requirements to matriculate to the next grade."

I took her advice, stayed the course, and prepared for the negative comments from the other students. When school finally started, and I ran into any of the parents, when the subject of whose classroom Brad was assigned to came up, I proudly told them Ms. Green's.

Ms. Green was a new teacher at the school. She was very energetic and academically demanding. She was also a dancer and yoga instructor outside of her day job, and she often asked the students to stand and stretch periodically during the day to relieve their restlessness.

It was a blessing to have Ms. Green as Brad's third grade teacher. She was a great teacher, and it was a good decision after all, developmentally, for him to repeat the third grade. With her encouragement, Brad performed his first dance scene on stage for an assembly. Reflecting back, I believe that this might have been the start of Brad's subsequent interest in dance.

At the end of the school year, several parents came up to me and admitted that they probably should have held their children back too, to help them "catch up," so to speak.

Sometimes as parents we need to put our pride aside and do what is best for our children.

The Awakening

THE DAY AFTER LABOR DAY in 2000, we finally made it to the long-awaited UCLA assessment appointment. I heard that people came from all over the world to get a diagnosis at the renowned medical center. The clinic provides inpatient as well as outpatient psychiatric and neurological therapy.

Dr. B. J. Freeman is a widely respected clinical psychologist in the field of autism. We were scheduled to see Dr. Freeman's assistant for our first appointment and we were told that we would meet with Dr. Freeman herself on the second visit.

I made sure that Brad and I arrived at our scheduled appointment on time. A friendly receptionist came out to greet us, and following behind her was Dr. Freeman's assistant. He introduced himself to Brad, and then, to my surprise, Dr. Freeman appeared. She informed me that her previous appointment had been cancelled, and she was able to meet with us after all.

Brad went with the assistant, and I went with Dr. Freeman into a room with a large, double-sided, mirrored window. I could see Brad interacting with the assistant in an adjoining room while Dr. Freeman interviewed me about his history and behavior. I was silently rooting him on, still hoping this was all a mistake.

I observed my son stumbling on some of the sequencing questions the assistant asked him. I would later learn that difficulty with sequential thought processing is one of the key characteristics of autism. Brad sat there with no expression, silent, not reacting or answering the questions. It was apparent that he had not passed the test, but I didn't know to what extent.

The next meeting was scheduled in two weeks, and my husband joined me there. At this meeting Dr. Freeman revealed to us that Brad had autism. Charles asked questions, and I took copious notes while she explained the test results and her findings.

Dr. Freeman said that she had known right away that our son probably had autism, because on our first meeting, before Brad greeted her, he had pointed out that she had forgotten to turn her calendar to September. She said that this was a dead giveaway to her, virtually confirming that his diagnosis was autism.

Brad has always been preoccupied with dates and birthdays. People with autism often perseverate on one subject; Brad's specific area of focus happens to be birthdays and dates. He can remember someone's birthdate from the moment he meets them and learns of their special day.

Dr. Freeman handed me a psychological report that was stamped in red ink: *AUTISM.* The last thing she said to me before we left her office was, "Don't be afraid of the label. It will open doors for you."

Later that evening I asked Charles how he felt about the diagnosis. He simply said, "It could be worse. We will work to provide him with a full life."

I felt like a ton of bricks had fallen on me; I was numbed and shocked. But I knew that now I could proceed to seek help for our son.

Armed with the information from Dr. Freeman, I was on a mission. All the frustration with schoolwork, the quirky behavior, playing alone, and what I had been labeling as 'shy' and 'quiet' now had a name and a diagnosis: AUTISM.

After receiving the formal diagnosis, the first person I called was my friend Dianne, who works in special education. She told me that she had suspected Brad might have autism, but hadn't been certain.

I sat there in silence, relieved that she seemed to agree with the experts at UCLA, but took in her words with trepidation. I wondered if she genuinely had not known for sure, or had she just wanted to protect me from the inevitable.

The next person I called with the bombshell news was my own mother. After I shared the terrible news about my son with her, she was very sympathetic, which comforted me greatly.

I was shocked, *and my world was* rocked *when my son was diagnosed with autism. I felt paralyzed down to my core. But Dr. Freeman's words of advice ignited my spirit and helped sustain me for many years to come.*

The Unfit Mother

Dr. Freeman referred me to Dr. Christine Ball, a speech pathologist specializing in language processing also at UCLA. After four visits she assessed Brad as having a severe *language processing disorder*. A language processing disorder is defined as having difficulty understanding others and expressing what you want to say.

Dr. Ball told me that Brad should have had intervention at four years old. He was then eight.

I felt like an unfit mother! Why hadn't I picked up on this before?

I had his hearing checked by his pediatrician at the age of five. Since he wasn't responding in what I felt was a timely manner, I thought that perhaps he couldn't hear me, but he said his hearing was fine.

His speech was understandable, although he didn't conduct long conversations about anything, which I thought was normal for what I figured was just a "shy, quiet type." I did notice, however, that when I spoke to him and pressed him for details, he would respond with "I don't know." What I hadn't realized was that he didn't have the words—the language expression or processing ability—to answer me.

I felt awful that I had been unaware there was a problem. As a consequence, my son had lost out on four years of therapy.

When you don't know, you just don't know. All you can do is to keep striving forward.

The Fishing Trip for Solutions

"Mission Impossible" was yet to begin. I was entering a world where all the rules for how to secure services successfully for a child with special needs are not clearly written or even known.

Everyone knows that when you are sick, you go to a hospital. Unfortunately, when you have a child with a developmental disability, it's not clear which remedy to try or where to get the help you need. It's like being out on a river with an oar but no compass.

This was the beginning of a very rude awaking. I soon discovered that I was entering a world that was not as compassionate as one might think, or at least hope.

Denna was one of many mothers I had volunteered with on school committees, and we had become good friends. She was a school nurse by profession, so when I received Brad's diagnosis I felt comfortable sharing it with her. Later she told me that her son had also been recommended for special education for a learning disability.

Denna and I made the decision to join forces to conquer the world of special needs. We both decided to take time off from work to learn more about special needs programs.

Although public schools are supported by public taxes and are primarily responsible for serving the educational needs of all children, including children with special needs, there is another category of schools in the world of education. These are called *non-public schools,* and they can provide children with more specialized and individual help not available in the public schools. We decided it was time to investigate these.

Denna and I started the first day by visiting Summit View, a nonpublic school for special needs students with learning disabilities of varying degrees and types. The school was located in Van Nuys, CA. Such schools operate separately from the public schools and are typically set up as nonprofit organizations. They are reimbursed by the school districts when the public schools are unable to meet a given student's needs. The costs of attending these schools can range up to $30,000 per year, depending on the needs of the individual child and the services provided. The classes offered are normally smaller, and in some cases the curriculum is individualized.

When we arrived at the front steps of the school, we stood outside the huge, ornamental metal gate and buzzed the admissions office. A voice spoke to us through the intercom, informing us that open-house hours were held on Wednesdays. Sadly, this was not a Wednesday.

We returned the following Wednesday for the open house and took a tour of the facility and the classrooms. Most of the students were more severely challenged than Brad, and I felt that the school was not a good fit for him.

By that day I had also added to my arsenal some information on special needs attorneys. We learned that many parents had to use special needs attorneys to secure services for their children. We decided that if this were the case for us, we weren't going to be caught short. I received the address and telephone number of a special needs attorney in the area, so our next stop was his office.

We spoke with a receptionist in the lobby, and she explained the services these attorneys provided. She told us that the first step was a consultation visit, which was necessary in order to schedule an appointment.

Onward and upward!

Our third stop was the Kelly Center. This was an educational program with a special reading-comprehension curriculum component. Ms. Washington, one of the teachers at Brad's school who had recommended it to us.

The executive director of the Kelly Center was a tall, blond, friendly woman named Susan Brown, who was dressed in a colorful bohemian-style skirt and peasant blouse. A beautiful, very large, black and brown German Shepherd lay on the floor near the leg of her chair. She told us that the dog was a source of comfort to her students.

I was impressed with the nurturing environment there, as it was vastly different from the other prescriptive environments, like the attorney's office and the grounds of the nonpublic school we had visited earlier. Ms. Brown invited us to sit in on some of the sessions in progress, to give us an idea of the Kelly Center's approach to reading comprehension.

I was also very impressed with the activities we saw. I knew instantly that Brad could benefit from the one-on-one attention and their "scaffold" approach to reading, which consisted of breaking down reading material into small parts for better understanding. After observing the program, I told her that I thought Brad would do well there.

Ms. Brown was initially a little bit apprehensive about taking my son as a client, because we did not yet have an IEP in place for him. IEP is the acronym for an *Individual Education Plan,* a written legal document generated by a school, that details all of the services and accommodations the school district will provide, along with the educational, behavioral, and counseling goals that have been set for each student with special needs.

When I got home, I faxed Brad's psychology report to her. After reviewing it, she agreed that Brad would be a good fit for the school, so I decided to wait for the upcoming IEP meeting to make a request for Brad to enroll in her program.

Ms. Brown also recommended Dr. William Takeshita, an optometrist who specializes in *vision perception therapy*, which evaluates how the brain processes and interprets visual information. Dr. Takeshita was a pioneer in this field of perception therapy at the time. He is now retired.

By this time Brad started a gymnastics class for children with special needs, provided by the regional center. Each state has its own agencies and criteria for delivering social services and programs to the developmentally disabled. In California there are 21 regional centers throughout the state that provide services for the developmentally disabled. The regional centers are individual non-profits funded by the state of California. Services offered through the regional center can start as early as birth and continue through adulthood.

Brad's gymnastics class was one of the many services offered through the regional center, that would help him to develop his gross motor skills and improve his coordination. Two weeks after my visit to the Kelly Center, during Brad's gymnastics class, I found myself in a conversation with another parent, Michelle, whose son was also in the class. She mentioned Dr. Takeshita and how great his therapy sessions were. I recognized the name as the same Dr. Takeshita that Ms. Brown had recommended previously.

I've always believed that when you hear something twice, you should act on it. I saw this as a sign and immediately followed up with a phone call. I left a message for Dr. Takeshita, saying that I was referred to him by the Kelly Center, and I received a speedy return call.

I made an appointment, and we went to see him. After two hours of testing he recommended forty hours of vision therapy for Brad.

We were making some good progress, but as I continued to put all the pieces together to understand the IEP process, I was still unsure as to who orchestrates all the diverse services.

I learned very quickly that, as the parent or caregiver, you oversee the programs and services, monitoring progress and making changes when necessary.

When you hear something twice along your journey, follow up on it. There are no accidents or coincidences. Synchronicity is God's way of speaking to us!

Finally Some Help

My friend Dianne, who is a special education teacher, recommended using what is known as a special education advocate. These advocates are familiar with the laws and educational protocols for special needs services and are invaluable assets. This type of advocate attends your annual or as needed, IEP meeting with you to assist in negotiating services and/or assessments that may be necessary. Brad's IEP date was coming up within a week, and Dianne highly recommended Elissa Henkin as an experienced and successful advocate.

I was feeling scared and desperate but ready to fight the whole way. I called Elissa three times and left messages but didn't get a return call. Time was running out—the date was approaching fast. Finally, I got a call back, and we arranged a consultation.

The day of our appointment I was prepared with copies of Brad's psychology report, speech evaluation, and vision perception assessment. I knocked on Elissa's door, very nervous and praying that she would take us as clients.

We met for an hour and a half, and she outlined what we would request at the IEP meeting. When I left the appointment, I was so happy that I wanted to jump up and down. I was finally able to turn this monstrous project over to a professional. What a relief!

I was so tired at this juncture that I didn't know what to do next. After I left our meeting, I found fifteen dollars in my purse and decided to celebrate with a steak dinner at a restaurant not far from Elissa's office.

Sometimes you just have to turn it over to a professional.

The IEP WAR: Ready to Fight

The day of the IEP meeting felt like going to war. It was an unusually hot day in January of 2001—a day to fight for the services that would make my child "normal"—and I was ready. I was nervous and felt queasy, but Elissa had reviewed the IEP process with us beforehand, and I was as prepared as I could be.

The meeting took place in a dimly lit auditorium-turned-conference-room where we all sat on folding chairs at a long wooden table. My husband was at my side. The psychologists, speech therapist, resource teachers, and Elissa were all in attendance.

The IEP took a total of eight grueling hours over the course of two days. It was so hot during the meetings that after four hours they gave us bottled water. We continued on the second day for an additional four hours, discussing occupational and vision therapy, technology, and a *one-on-one assistant.*

A one-on-one assistant was someone who would shadow Brad all day, helping him with his work and keeping him on track academically. The IEP team argued that the classes were small, so he did not need a one-on-one assistant. Elissa quickly pointed out that the size of the class was irrelevant to the needs of the student.

I was so very glad that I had Elissa to help us. I researched information on the internet about teaching children with autism and passed that around to the IEP team, but if I had been at the meeting by myself, I would not have been familiar with the legal protocols that needed to be followed. For instance, parents should have copies of all of the assessments and reports related to their children. In this case, I had not been given a copy of a report from the initial SST (Student Success Team) meeting. This report was passed out among the school staff and discussed in a sidebar conversation without our input. Elissa observed actions the team had taken that were not in compliance with the process, and she brought those to their attention.

The results of the IEP were that Brad would receive a one-on-one assistant, speech therapy three times a week, resource services, which meant additional help from a certified teacher other than his primary teacher; and added modifications to his instruction, such as books on tape, a permanent seat in the front of the classroom, additional time to complete tasks, a slant board for handwriting improvement and vision therapy. The reading program from the Kelly Center was not granted, but I was assured that with the other services, the reading comprehension problem would be addressed. I was ecstatic at the outcome of the meeting, and I breathed a sigh of relief.

Note to parents:

> *I learned early on that parents must be organized. It is essential to organize your documents for easy accessibility. Those assessments are often your best justification for requesting services. Have ready any assessments done by the school or your providers. The IEPs in each school district may be formatted differently, but they all have the same basic components. Keep*

all your assessments and IEP documents in a three-ring binder with dividers labeled for each section:

SECTION I

1) Assessments (psychology, speech evaluations, and behavior assessments; vision assessment, occupational therapy assessment, etc.)
2) IEP copies
3) Correspondence from a) schools and b) regional centers
4) Health paperwork (doctors' reports, physical examinations, etc.)
5) Samples of schoolwork
6) Copy of school district rights

SECTION II
Before the IEP meeting, you and your advocate or attorney must decide what your goals are and what you want to accomplish. Have the following prepared in advance:

1) The services you want your child to receive
2) The preferred frequency of those services

We were finally on our way to receiving the services Brad so desperately needed.

The Do-Over

In February of 2001, the new semester began with a clean slate. Brad had already started the third grade in Ms. Green's class in the fall, but now he would be able to continue with his new services in place, which we had acquired at the IEP meeting.

On the first day of class I waited anxiously to meet Brad's new one-on-one assistant, Ms. Lindsey. From a distance, I heard the distinctive voice of a woman making her way down the hallway. She definitely had a big personality.

Ms. Lindsay had worked in public schools for many years as a one-on-one assistant to special education students. She was mature, positive, nurturing, had a no-nonsense attitude, and was forthright in her demeanor. She was confident, with a can-do spirit that I liked right away. Ms. Lindsey would assist Brad in understanding and completing the assignments as well as serve as a liaison between the administration and me, communicating any information regarding Brad that I might need to know.

We discussed how she was to communicate with me, via a daily log. The communication log would consist of Brad's classwork and homework assignments and would include a comments section for any behavioral or social concerns. After our meeting, I felt certain that Brad would be in capable hands.

In third grade, Brad's handwriting was illegible. He was unorganized and couldn't keep up with his assignments. To help him with organization and handwriting, the IEP provided him with a graphic organizer and a slant board. The slant board functioned similar to a ruler, to help students who have difficulty writing in a straight line.

On a more personal note, Brad didn't really know how to smile and he was socially awkward. He would often repeat lines from movie soundtracks, and he could not converse with classmates in an age-appropriate manner.

Repeating lines or words from movies is a form of *echolalia*. Some children with autism repeat lines from movies or television to calm themselves. Doing this frequently, however, he was soon labeled "weird" by the other students in his class.

Under Ms. Lindsey's tutelage, however, I saw significant improvements in Brad's academic performance and social development. He was self-motivated in completing both his classwork and his homework assignments. With the use of his slant board, his handwriting improved, becoming much more legible.

Ms. Lindsey was also instrumental in teaching him how to express himself socially. He even learned how to smile and laugh, and he started to play with the other students on the schoolyard. He started telling his classmates that he wanted to play with them during recess and lunchtime. Brad was learning how to play basketball, bringing his own ball from home, and initiating pickup games with the other boys in his class.

During this time Brad entered a district sponsored speech contest in which he won first place. Ms. Lindsay worked with him tirelessly on his speech. Along with Ms. Lindsey, my mother, my aunt, and I were there to support him on the day of the competition.

This was a huge turning point in Brad's progress. This single event gained Brad the respect of his classmates and peers.

At the end of every school year, the students were given a required, standardized SAT-9 test, and I opted for Brad not to take it, fearing that he wouldn't perform well. Instead, Ms. Lindsay encouraged me to let Brad take the test so that, in her words, "he won't feel like an outcast."

I agreed to let him take the test. Afterwards I had to concede that I was wrong in my thinking, and she was right. He performed at proficient levels in some areas, and taking the test boosted his self-confidence tremendously.

After some reflection, I have realized that having his one-on-one assistant, Ms. Lindsey, was the most important service that Brad received.

Ms. Lindsey was Brad's one-on-one assistant for three and a half years. She empowered both Brad and myself. I became acquainted with some of his previously unseen cognitive abilities, particularly with math computations and spelling proficiency.

It can be difficult to trust someone else's opinion of what is best for your child—especially when it may differ vastly from yours—but there will be times when their opinion is exactly what you need to hear.

The Bigger World of Autism

DURING THIS TIME, I ATTENDED my first autism conference at Pasadena City College. The whole world of autism was new and intriguing, and now I was part of it.

I found myself circling in a whirlwind of activity, feeling raw, vulnerable, and numb from being bombarded with all the information at the conference events. It was overwhelming.

I met parents who had children with limited or no speech, and I felt fortunate and so sad for them. One couple in their thirties told me about their four-year-old daughter who had recently been assessed and diagnosed at the regional center. They had to come to terms with their child being diagnosed as developmentally delayed, but I could tell that they were still in shock and dealing with the trauma.

I listened as the young mother's voice cracked when she shared their story with me. Their child was unable to feed herself, could not determine depth perception when playing in a sandbox, and would fall while walking. My heart went out to them.

I attended a workshop entitled *Conservatorship and Trusts: How Is Your Child Going to Be Cared For After You, the Parent, Are Gone?* I had never really given much thought to who would care for Brad when Charles and I were no longer around, and it brought up a new aspect of our lives to think about.

Vendors were everywhere, selling everything from flashcards and games to diet supplements and books. Notices were posted for advocacy groups and special programs and more.

A *Walk for Autism* booth advertised a 5K to raise money for research. I had mixed feelings about it. My heart moved me to reach for the brochure and perhaps participate, but I was hesitant about taking it or any of the colorful buttons because, in my mind, that would have been a confirmation that I had a child with autism.

As I sat in the dark in the large auditorium, waiting for the next speaker to arrive, I struck up a conversation with a woman sitting next to me. She shared with me that she had just received Social Security benefits for her daughter. I was not aware that a child with a diagnosis of autism was eligible for Social Security benefits.

The woman on the other side of me was a special ed teacher whose son had an attention deficit disorder also known as (ADD). She admitted to me that she didn't want him labeled.

I told her, "Don't be afraid of the label. The label will open doors for you." I thought for a moment after I said it, and remembered how I had felt when those words were spoken to me. It was hard to accept at first, but after a while, I embraced them, and I felt sure she would too.

Diagnoses of autism have grown exponentially. As of this writing, according to the Centers for Disease Control (CDC), one in 68 children in the US are eventually diagnosed with autism, as compared with only one in 150 just fifteen years ago, when my son Brad was first diagnosed.

The Good-Looking Kid

I GUESS AS PARENTS WE deal with our grief about our children's conditions in many different ways.

One Saturday afternoon when Brad was nine, I was sitting at his gymnastics class talking to Kathy, the mother of one of the other students with autism. Brad and Kathy's son, Bruce, had befriended each other.

She said, "At least Bruce is a good-looking kid, even though he has autism."

He *was* a good-looking kid, I agreed.

Bruce was an only child. Kathy shared with me that they didn't have any other family living in Los Angeles and that their closet relative was in Northern California. After observing the two boys getting along well during the class, I agreed to arrange a play date and invited Bruce over to our house.

When Bruce arrived, he and Brad played basketball outside for a while and seemed to be enjoying themselves. The two of them later came in the house, and the door slammed quite loud. The next thing I knew, Bruce was jumping up and down on my living room couch. He was scared, and I didn't know what to do. I tried talking him off of the couch and found myself getting upset when it didn't seem to be working. I felt helpless that I did not know how to console him.

That was the last time we invited anyone else with autism to our house. After that incident, I was afraid that a parent or caregiver might forget to inform me of any idiosyncratic or life threatening behavior that I needed to be aware of while they were in my care.

After that experience, I felt that prejudice against my son's "own kind" had overtaken me. I could then empathize if someone else did not feel comfortable having Brad at their house. But Brad was different, I would tell myself.

I envisioned that my own friends' children who were Brad's age would naturally become his friends, but that was not to be. This was painful, but I had to accept the fact that I was on my own when it came to finding friends for Brad.

A Friend in Need

In his sixth-grade year, Brad took part in a summer program. A showcase at the end of the summer was held for parents in which the students danced, sang, and performed skits. Afterwards we were invited to have refreshments.

Dominique was a chubby, friendly boy Brad had met in the program. Brad introduced me to his friend and to Dominique's parents. We exchanged phone numbers and promised to keep in touch and get the boys together soon.

I picked up Dominique a few times and took he and Brad to Color Me Mine, a paint-your-own-pottery studio, to basketball games, the park, and the museum. The two boys seemed to have a good time together.

The last time I arranged to pick up Dominique, I called before we left our house, but when we got to his house, no one was home. We sat in the car and I continued calling, thinking maybe there had been a misunderstanding about the time. I finally gave up calling, and we drove back home.

We never saw Dominique again. I could only speculate what might have happened. Maybe Brad had been repeating some lines from a movie or showing signs of his disability, and the family hadn't known how to deal with his behavior.

Socializing, making and maintaining friendships can be difficult for individuals with autism. I carefully explained to Brad what might have happened and that he could now focus on making new friends. This incident afforded an opportunity for a teachable moment for Brad.

This was another defeat in the search to find a friend for Brad, but it was an important lesson he learned about making friends and finding new ones. Be resilient!!

The Big Move

It was the beginning of his eighth grade year, Brad had been attending the charter school for five years when I became unhappy with the inconsistent speech and occupational therapy sessions he was receiving there. The charter schools subcontract special ed therapy services from private companies. His sessions were often cancelled, and there was a high turnover in personnel. I was nervous about moving Brad from the small charter school campus to the large neighborhood middle school. Then, I was very concerned about him being able to navigate the large middle school campus. To make matters worse, Brad was having trouble socially at the charter school. The students were making fun of him, and he was falling behind academically. I decided to enroll him at the neighborhood middle school for the summer session to give him time to familiarize himself with the new campus before the fall semester started. This move also helped me to adjust to the change before school started. I found out that one of our neighbors was a teacher at the middle school, and I spoke with her. She told me the school had a good special education department. That was all I needed to hear to confirm my decision.

With the IEP in place for the new year, Brad was entitled to transportation. The school bus picked him up from home and dropped him off at school. This was Brad's first experience taking a school bus for special ed students.

I made arrangements for the school bus to take him to Chace Hills playground after his summer school classes. I was very nervous about him taking the school bus, though, because I wasn't sure if he would be able to find his counselor at the park once he was dropped off. I then made arrangements with the park staff for someone to meet him when the bus dropped him off and take him to his counselor.

Everything worked out that summer, and Brad transitioned to the new environment successfully; but when September came, I wasn't sure what to expect.

Up to that point, Brad had been in a traditional classroom setting with a one-on-one assistant. At the new middle school, without my prior knowledge, he was placed in an autism class. In this class all the students in the classroom had autism, with varying degrees of severity.

This was the first time Brad had been in a class with only students with autism, and most of them were much more physically challenged than he was. Upon visiting the class for the first time, I was startled to see that some of the students moved around the classroom lethargically, some paced, and others drooled. Brad would ask me almost daily, "What's wrong with those kids, Mom?"

I was also unaware that he had automatically been placed in an adaptive physical education class, along with the rest of the students with autism. This class was designed specifically for severely physically handicapped children.

After about three weeks into the semester, Ms. Jones, the instructor, caught my attention one morning and told me that he didn't need to be in her class. She explained that she taught only the very basic fundamentals of movement, such as running and jumping.

By that time, Brad was already a pretty good athlete. He was taking taekwondo classes and playing in a basketball league at the local park. I realized that the class was not the best environment for Brad at this stage. I called for an emergency IEP meeting to have him transferred out of adaptive P.E. and the autism class and mainstreamed into typical classes with a one-on-one assistant.

After writing a letter requesting the change, I waited six weeks for this meeting to be scheduled. I later learned the emergency IEP meeting should have happened within thirty days. This was very frustrating and was yet another example of the bureaucratic problems in the system.

One of the main obstacles to placing Brad in a traditional classroom with a one-on-one assistant was Ms. Cook, his autism classroom teacher. She didn't want Brad to be transferred out of her class. Ms. Cook was very controlling and told me that she had the power to hold him back a year if I did not concede to her wishes to leave him in her class.

I took her words as a direct threat to impede my son's progress, and I was determined to prevent her from wielding that kind of power over him. I moved forward with my request to have him placed in regular classes with a one-on-one assistant, as he had been previously.

During this process, I learned that LAUSD was legally obligated to respond to written requests within certain time frames. I also learned that Brad could receive collaborative instruction, in which some of his classes would be smaller, and the students study the same material as in a traditional class but at a slower pace. On the other hand, he could still be mainstreamed in his elective studies, such as art and physical education, where he would take classes with the regular school population. This way he could have the best of both worlds.

Sometimes you just have to move through your fear and do it anyway.

The Accuser

One February morning, Ms. Cook called our house stating, "There is a problem." She went on to accuse Brad of drawing a disturbing picture of an angry, fat lady with her hair standing up on top of her head. The caption under the drawing read, *I will assassinate Ms. Wilson.* It was assumed to represent one of the classroom aides, whose name was Ms. Wilson.

The next day my husband went to the school and asked to see the drawing in question. He had Brad write something on a piece of paper and showed Ms. Cook that Brad's handwriting did not match the handwriting on the drawing, nor did Brad know the meaning of the word *assassinate,* which was not part of his vocabulary.

Charles told me he had an intuition that Mr. Jacob, Brad's one-on-one assistant, might have done this. He then asked Mr. Jacob to write something.

Mr. Jacob finally admitted to drawing the picture in question and writing the caption. He claimed he did this because he was romantically interested in Ms. Wilson, and she had rejected his advances. Charles asked him why he was willing to let Brad take the blame for his actions. He apologized and said that he had been very angry when he had drawn the picture and written the caption.

This would not be the first time Mr. Jacob displayed misconduct on the job.

This was another fight for the "cause." Our son needed our voices to support him when others did not and when he was unable to speak for himself.

The Audition

MY COUSIN "CE" TOLD ME about an acting school in which she was enrolling her daughter, who was Brad's age. I thought it would be a good experience for him to learn how to act and perhaps dance and sing. Children had to audition in order to participate in the program, so Charles and I picked out a short speech for Brad to practice for his audition.

Parents weren't allowed to be present during the audition, but afterwards, we reconvened with the teacher and she told us that Brad had simply recited random lines from various movies. Brad was very much into movies, and he habitually repeated dialogue whenever he felt nervous or didn't know what else to say.

The executive director of the program met with us later. She told us, "I'm sorry, but I can't work with your son or teach him anything."

Charles and I were devastated as we drove home in silence. It felt like we had just been slapped down from yet another chance for our son to be included in a typical childhood experience. This was another blow confirming that we did, indeed, have a son with special needs.

We were nearly paralyzed by strong emotions as I told Brad that he hadn't passed the audition. His response was unemotional; he only seemed puzzled about the whole event.

Not one to give up easily, I was determined to find a school that would take him. About Talented Kids was another local performing arts school, and I was relieved to learn that Brad would not need to audition to participate. He was accepted and enjoyed a three-month program of acting, dancing, and singing.

At the end of the program, there was a final performance. I was so excited and proud of him that I invited all my friends to come to see him perform. He and his partner danced in a piece entitled "Jitterbug." Some of the better dancers were positioned in front of them, but I didn't care. I was happy to see my son on stage and holding his own.

After the performance, I was so excited that I rushed to find Frances, the program director. I found her in the parking lot, packing her car. Tears of joy and heartfelt appreciation streamed down my face, and I thanked her profusely for allowing Brad to have such a great experience and for working with him. She told me that Brad was a pleasure to have in the program.

Someone had taken a chance and allowed my son to enjoy a wonderful experience, and I was very grateful. *On the road to feeling normal* became my new mantra.

As a parent of a child with special needs, you will always have one foot in the "normal world" and the other foot in the special needs world. Finding balance is knowing when to push for a normal experience and when to advocate for special needs support.

The Temp

Mr. Jacob was still Brad's one-on-one assistant when he transitioned from middle school to high school, and I was grateful that Brad had his help. One day, however, I got a phone call from Ms. Frost, one of the vice principals at the school. She expressed concern that Mr. Jacob had been seen approaching and flirting with some of the girls at the school. She said that this behavior was inappropriate and that Mr. Jacob would be dismissed immediately. She assured me that the school would replace him and that it would happen soon.

I totally agreed with her decision but wondered where this would leave my son. I was very concerned, because I didn't think Brad could navigate a large high school campus on his own; including getting to classes on time, keeping up with all of the in-class and homework assignments, and making it to his speech therapy sessions. I was not surprised about Mr. Jacob's dismissal, especially after he had tried to shift the blame to Brad for his bad behavior in middle school; however, he had been a helpful support for Brad in getting around the campus, and now that was in jeopardy.

Ms. Frost called me a few days later and said that an assistant named Ms. Perry would be replacing Mr. Jacob temporarily. Ms.

Perry had years of experience working with special education students at the elementary schools, but this would be her first assignment with a high school student.

When I met her, she struck me as very enthusiastic, patient, and professional. I felt certain that she would be a good fit for Brad.

My guess was correct. With Ms. Perry's help, Brad's growth and personal development took off exponentially.

Ms. Perry was poised and showed a great deal of proficiency in determining when to assist Brad and when to allow him to express his independence and utilize his own problem-solving skills. She was even wise strategically in choosing where she stood or sat in the classroom so that Brad could feel a sense of independence while always making sure that she was visible and available if he needed her.

Ms. Perry was a tremendous advocate for Brad, both in and outside of the classroom. For example, she was able to handle an incident in a photography class where the students were assigned specific seats. When Brad arrived at the classroom, another student had intentionally sat in his seat to provoke him. Brad's non-confrontational manner prevented his complaining about it. He just let the other student remain in his assigned seat and began to look for another seat

When Ms. Perry arrived and saw the situation, she quickly intervened and coached Brad on how to tell the student to find another seat. Brad did as instructed, and the student moved without making a scene.

Another incident when Ms. Perry advocated for Brad was in a cooking class. The instructor didn't want Brad to use a knife to chop vegetables, although she allowed the other students to use the knives. Ms. Perry observed a lot of dangerous horse-play with the knives by the other students in the classroom, and she told the instructor, "It's not Brad that you should be worried about; it is the so-called 'normal' students who are behaving irresponsibly with the knives." The instructor then allowed Brad to use a knife to cut up his vegetables, along with the rest of the class.

Ms. Perry opened up Brad's world by encouraging him to try new classes, taste new foods, and have new experiences.

Establishing viable partnerships that align with your values is a powerful strategy.

Fifteenth Birthday

By his fifteenth birthday, it had been a while since Brad had had a party, and I decided it was time. When I asked him what kind of party he wanted, he said that he would like a roller skating party.

I decided to teach him how to plan a party. My first instruction for him was to put together a list of the friends he wanted to invite. He seemed to be more social in general at that point, and I was hopeful that he had made some friends in school that he could ask to attend.

I designed an invitation for him on the computer, and the next day he gave out invitations to the ten school "friends" he had named. This time I thought that he had finally done it, found some friends on his own.

On the day of the party I ordered food and decorations, and we set off for the skating rink. Some family members and other friends had also been invited and met us there, including my daughter and a few of her friends.

After about an hour and a half, Brad started asking where the friends that he had invited from school were.

I suggested, "Let's go out to the lobby to see if they are standing in line and trying to get into the rink."

We went to look, and there was a long line outside, but no one in our party was there. Brad was disappointed, and so was I.

A few minutes after we went back to the rink, the one person who appeared to be more than just a "friend from school" arrived. Kirsten was a cute, slender girl dressed in stylishly tight jeans. She told us that she had left work early to come to the party and that she did not want to miss it because Brad had invited her.

After her arrival, Brad forgot all about the other people that he had invited who hadn't shown up. He and Kirsten skated together like a couple of pros. Brad's friend Isaaq finally arrived late and asked Brad who Kirsten was, and he replied, "She is just a friend." To me, she seemed heaven-sent.

I knew my son pretty well and as I predicted, the following Monday the so-called school friends whom he had given the invitations received a third-degree interrogation. He asked them what had happened and why they hadn't shown up. When he came home, he reported back to me the lame excuses each one had given him for not coming to his party.

Brad was on his way to advocating for himself, and I was proud of him.

The Confidence Builders

WITH MUCH PRACTICE AND DEDICATION over time, Brad had perfected his basketball skills and was proud of his great jump shot. In the summer before his freshman year, Brad tried out for the varsity basketball team. He did not make it and was very upset. A short time after tryouts, I learned that the school was a veritable city basketball powerhouse winning many city championship titles. I didn't realize how skilled you had to be to make the varsity team. Ultimately, in his junior year a better opportunity became available for him to apply for what is known as the "team manager" to the varsity basketball team. These "team managers" can sometimes be special ed students. Their duties are to supply the players with towels and water during the games.

I then spoke with the basketball coach, and after a few recommendations in his favor, Brad was selected to be the team manager for the basketball team during his junior year. We traveled to several other schools where away-games were played, and it was a wonderful experience for him. It was mutually beneficial for Brad and for his peers on the team: the team members were able to understand his disability and maintain a relationship with him, while Brad learned additional social skills, such as how to maintain friendships and become more socially accepted in school.

Other elective classes he was able to enjoy included a web-design class and a drama-production class. He even learned to play golf. With Ms. Perry's support, Brad was able to have a positive and full high school experience.

In a relatively short time he became more responsible, learning his way around the high school campus and staying on task to finish his assignments. He kept track of his homework, asked and answered questions, and became a viable part of class discussions.

During his senior year, Ms. Perry once again championed his cause, encouraging his teachers to assign him a position as a student worker, in which he delivered messages and packages to various departments across the campus. Ms. Perry was a great asset and a believer in Brad furthering his education beyond high school so that he could eventually gain his independence and live a full life.

Fortunately Ms. Perry's "temporary" stay was extended to four years. During this time I found that her values and her hopes and dreams for Brad were identical to my own, and I will be eternally grateful for the time she spent with him.

Extracurricular activities will help to socialize children.

Running Track in High School

Brad had always been interested in running as a sport, and over the previous few years he and I had run in local 5K and 10k charity fundraisers. We once ran a race in nearby Orange County, where he won first place in his age group, so I thought it would be a good idea for him to try out for the high school track team.

During his sophomore and junior years, we had missed the deadlines for track tryouts, so I was on the lookout for announcements in early December during his senior year. I asked Ms. Perry to make sure that Brad went to the information meeting, which was mandatory. He made it there and later gave me the dates for the tryouts.

On the scheduled dates it rained cats and dogs! I asked Charles to double check in case the tryouts were cancelled and, if so, to find out when they would be rescheduled. He learned that they were rescheduled for different dates.

Charles took Brad to the tryouts on the rescheduled dates, but no one was at the track when they arrived. They came home confused and disappointed, wondering what happened.

Winter break came and went. In the new year I followed up with the track coach, and she informed me that the tryouts had taken place during the winter break. "All the team members have already been selected," she said.

My guess was that we were deliberately misinformed about the rescheduled dates and times. I begged her to give my son a chance, since he had not gotten an opportunity to try out. She refused but added, "If I decide to have another tryout, I will announce it over the PA."

I explained that Brad might not hear it and asked if she could she let me know instead. She declined and wouldn't budge. I was fuming when I left her room, but once again I was determined to make this experience happen for Brad.

I mentioned the dilemma to a friend, and she told me about the L.A. Jets, a community track team. I rushed home and got on the computer to find the team's contact information. I called them and learned that they were holding tryouts in two days.

The timing was perfect! Two days later, Charles took Brad to the park, where he tried out for and made the team. He ended up participating in the 200, 400, and 800 meter races.

The highlight of his time with the L.A. Jets was a trip to a regional track meet in Phoenix, Arizona.

I was comfortable by this time making my concerns known to the administration, but you have to know when to pick your battles. I chose not to fight this particular one because the goal was simply to get Brad on a track team, and I found a way to sign him up for the community track team, which turned out to be very fulfilling for Brad and our family in the long run.

Looking Ahead Beyond High School

MOST HIGH SCHOOLS OFFER TWO educational tracks for special ed students: They can choose between the *diploma track* and the *certificate of completion track*. Students on the certificate of completion track are allowed to stay in the school district and receive services until the age of twenty-two. On the certificate of completion-track students receive a certificate but not an official diploma. We chose the diploma track for Brad.

As of the date of this writing, special ed students in California are not required to pass the California High School Exit Exam (CAHSEE) to receive a diploma. When Brad was in school, however, the diploma track required taking classes and also passing the CAHSEE.

At that time only 13% of students in special ed classes passed the CAHSEE, and Brad was one of them. He completed his classes and passed the exit exam successfully. Before Brad left high school we enrolled him in an English class for disabled students at West Los Angeles College, a nearby community college.

During his last semester in high school, Brad participated in the Workability Program, a school-district program designed to give students with disabilities an opportunity to experience the world of employment. He got a job at a local pharmacy, stocking merchandise and maintaining the shelves. Being able to work and earn a paycheck was a big boost to his confidence.

These were precious moments when I was beginning to feel more and more "normal." Knowing that Brad was accomplishing goals like any typically developing teenager made me beam from ear to ear!

Hell to Work

While Brad was still in high school, I enrolled him in a pilot partnership program that allowed special education students to work on a nearby university campus. Unfortunately, he did not qualify because the program director changed the criteria for the selection process after we had turned in the application packet. I made sure to take my complaints to the special ed district office and revealed how the selection process was flawed and explained the reasons why. As serendipity would have it, the department head referred me to another more established and historically successful program, the Workability Program.

Brad was a part of the Workability Program during his last semester of high school. Before Brad could start, however, Ms. Perry had to receive mobility training—formal instruction on how to use public transportation—because she and Brad were going to be taking a city bus from the school to the job site at the pharmacy.

Ms. Perry's attempts to attend the three-hour mobility training were met with a series of cancelled appointments from the school district's staff. After two months of phone calls from me about this situation, she finally got the training, and Brad was ready to go to work. But before he could start, the work-experience teacher at the school had to provide customer service training for Brad.

On a sunny afternoon in a brightly lit but cramped room, the training began. I sat next to Brad at a long student desk, and Ms. Nash, the work-experience teacher, sat across from him. A student with a laptop computer was sitting at the end of the table doing his homework.

Ms. Nash began asking Brad general questions about customer service. Her first question to Brad was, "If a customer came to you and looked like they needed some help, what would you say?"

Brad replied, "I would say, may I help you?"

She stared at him for a split second with a frown and then reprimanded him, saying, "Brad, you should not curse at the customers!"

I had been sitting right next to him and quickly asked, "What do you think he said?"

She answered, "He said, 'Hell, I cannot help you.' "

The student using his laptop at the table said that he heard Brad use a curse word, as well.

Brad sometimes speaks in a low, almost inaudible voice, and his words are occasionally misunderstood, but I was in disbelief that this kind of misunderstanding was happening. I explained that he had said, "May I HELP you?"

Ms. Nash accepted my explanation and was relieved that he had not in fact used a curse word.

This was yet another situation when advocating for my son was absolutely necessary. I hesitate to imagine what would have happened if I had not been present. This misunderstanding could have jeopardized his opportunity to gain valuable work experience.

The Champagne Party

It was the Spring of 2009, it was prom time and Brad had already attended his senior prom. As tradition has evolved this is the season to attend many champagne parties for the high school graduates. We had plans on attending a champagne party for one of a family friend's daughter. Because we were running late, Brad and I rushed to get over there.

A champagne party is a newer celebratory concept that has grown in popularity over recent years. Basically, it's a gathering for family and friends to see prom attendees off on their first official formal outing.

A family friend, Debbie, was having a champagne party for her daughter Erica's prom. Erica had been very active at the Fame Conservatory, the same drama camp where Brad had auditioned and had been rejected years earlier.

The party was festive, with drinks and all kind of hors d'oeuvres and other foods. After Erica's date arrived, most of the guests moved outside to see the young couple drive off. Just a few of us were left in the house when Brad spotted someone he thought he recognized and started to talk to her.

I was relaxing in a corner, enjoying a bottled water and watching Brad. He and the young woman were standing nearby, and the executive director of the Fame Conservatory sat near them.

The director turned to Brad and said, "I know you from somewhere, but I don't recall where."

I spoke up. "He auditioned for your conservatory years ago, and you rejected him, and since then he has been in three dramatic performances. I found a wonderful school that could teach him, which you said was something you were not able to do."

She replied, "So you are you putting me on blast?"

"Yes, I am," I admitted.

She searched the room frantically for a comforting kindred soul, but no one was there to rescue her.

This lone incident allowed me to feel avenged regarding an injustice I felt had been perpetrated upon my child. It's said that revenge is sweet, although perhaps not always advised, but it's also a truism that mothers typically have an unquenchable instinct to protect their children.

Don't let people with big titles deter you from your goal, because a lot of them are really just small-minded.

Don't sweat the small stuff! It will come around again, so just know that injustice will be avenged.

Tap Dancing

At eighteen, after many years of requests, Brad finally had the time to take tap dancing lessons. I never knew where this interest had come from, but maybe he'd seen it in a movie. Over the years, he was involved in so many other therapies and activities that he just never had time to pursue it.

We located an established tap school, and he started taking classes there. He loved it. He practiced at home all the time, and it was great to see him so happy. Every Tuesday night I would take him to class and wait in the lobby until it was over.

He had been going to the studio for two months when one particular evening we arrived a little early. The receptionist beckoned me over and told me that there had been an issue with Brad the previous week. She said that apparently Brad asked Pam, the tap dance instructor, to touch his "thing."

I was appalled and couldn't believe what she was telling me. Then I thought to myself, *He's eighteen, so maybe he did say it.*

I promptly went outside to where Brad was sitting and waiting for class to start and asked him if he had said those words.

He was as surprised as I was and asked, "Who said that about me? Do they want me kicked out of this school?"

I told him to go to class and that I would handle it. This was the very reason that I typically stayed at the school, to avoid any incidents, but I guessed that it hadn't worked.

After class, I asked Pam if there was a problem the previous week. She went on to tell me a story similar to the receptionist's report.

I relayed to her the misunderstanding that had taken place at school during the work training, when the teacher and a student thought Brad had said something that he clearly had not. I emphasized that I was present and had witnessed the incident myself. I then asked her if the music was on, and she said that it was. I informed her of Brad's history of speaking in a low voice and sometimes not clearly enunciating his words. Allowing for the distraction of the loud music playing at the time, she conceded that perhaps she hadn't heard what she'd thought.

Another day ADVOCATING for my son....

I cannot stress enough how imperative it is to be on the lookout for these types of incidents, accepting that these situations can happen and that this is part of having a child with special needs.

The Big Celebration

I WAS SEARCHING FOR AN appropriate way to recognize Brad's high school accomplishments and to thank all the people who had helped us support him along his journey. We couldn't do this the way most teenagers celebrate rites of passage, such as getting a driver's license or going solo on a first date, etc.

Since we could not have a typical "graduation party" without a crowd of school friends, I decided we would have a teacher-appreciation luncheon at a large popular restaurant in conjunction with Autism Awareness Month. This party would include some of Brad's high school teachers, significant teachers from lower and middle school, counselors, tutors, dance instructors, speech therapists, a gymnastics instructor, acting teachers, advocates, and anyone else who had played a role in his success.

All told, we wanted to recognize fifty honorees. We decided that we would invite friends and family, as well, and fill the room with a total of one hundred supporters.

Brad was very excited about the event. He dressed in a navy blue suit with his embroidered 2009 graduation sash and looked quite dapper.

Outside the restaurant entrance, he greeted and directed all of his guests into the private ballroom. Inside, our "committee" rushed around frantically, making last-minute preparations while guests filed in.

A designated table was laden with photos of Brad and memorabilia from his participation in track, tap dancing, cooking, and singing classes. A video camera was set up to capture every minute of this memorable event.

Brad's friend Isaaq played jazz on the electric guitar, while his cousin prepared for an interpretive dance performance set to Brad's favorite song, arranged as a special part of the program. Also on the program was the deputy to our U.S. Congressional Representative, Maxine Waters, who would speak on behalf of the Congresswoman.

Our daughter, Brittany, was the mistress of ceremonies, but the program started out with a few words from me, sharing with the audience the reasons why this event was so important to Charles and myself.

"Teachers are rarely acknowledged publicly by parents for all their hard work," I began. I stressed that it was this "village" that was responsible for Brad's success.

The main part of the celebration was Brad's personal acknowledgment of the fifty honorees. Each of them stood at their seats when Brad called their names. He then coupled the introductions with one thing he'd learned from each one and thanked them graciously.

Brad has always had a gift of memorizing lines and facts with ease, and he had memorized every tribute he had written for each of the honorees. This just goes to show that when you get short-changed in one area, God often gifts you with other extraordinary skills.

Charles then presented each honoree with congressional commendations from the state, city, and county and a plaque featuring Brad's photo, with the words *Thank You for All That You Have Done* inscribed on the front.

The grand finale was Brad's surprise presentation to Ms. Perry. Brad acknowledged her by asking her to come to the podium, and there he read a speech he had written, thanking her for all she had done for him and for the many things she had taught him.

He read his speech to her in Farsi, Ms. Perry's native tongue. Brad had first written the speech, and her son had recorded it in Farsi. I had then written out the Farsi translation phonetically for Brad to read aloud to her.

This was by far the highlight of the afternoon. Ms. Perry was overjoyed, and this was a proud moment for her. She started crying, and I joined her with tears of my own.

Afterwards there were remarks from the attendees, acknowledging Brad's achievements, and then photos were taken. An article covering the event appeared in the local paper, and a press release was sent to LAUSD's media department and television station. We later received a congratulatory letter from President Obama, as well.

The day after the presentation, at school, all of Brad's teachers in attendance at the celebration were the envy of the other teachers who had not been part of it. As a family, we viewed the celebration as a huge success—to be given the opportunity to express our deepest gratitude to those who had been at his side throughout his education.

I felt that, in the end, we really did have our GRADUATION PARTY!

We can have the same kinds of celebrations as other families, and although they may look a little different, we can achieve the same results in the end.

Forty Days and Forty Nights

EIGHT WEEKS BEFORE HIGH SCHOOL was to end, we were skating quickly downhill with LAUSD. With only forty school days left, I had thought that all my advocating and fighting was coming to an end when I received a disturbing phone call. I was informed that they were reassigning Ms. Perry and pairing Brad with someone new.

He passed the CAHSEE, and he was a LAUSD "success case," so why would they want to change things now? I wondered.

I met with the recently appointed special education coordinator at the school and informed her that Ms. Perry had been with Brad for four years and had been instrumental in his passing the last two classes in order to graduate, and he would not have time to adjust to someone new. This coordinator didn't know Brad, nor was she familiar with the details of his circumstances, but she heard me out and then assured me that there wouldn't be any changes.

For two days I anxiously awaited her phone call. Finally I called her, and she said that she had forgotten to phone me, but informed me that Ms. Perry's assignment with Brad would *not* be changing.

This was the last battle in high school, and I was very happy to put it behind me and move forward.

Remember, don't ever think you can rest. You must be ready to fight to the very end!

We Made It!

Graduation Day was approaching, and Brad participated in all the senior activities connected with graduating, such as Beach Day and his prom. For my part, I just wanted to make sure that all of Brad's books had been returned and all his fees were paid. With all the activities and the excitement of his impending graduation, mental exhaustion soon consumed me, but there was no way I could stop now when the big payoff was just around the corner.

Reflecting on our partnership with Ms. Perry and the community of people that helped Brad to have a successful high school experience made me smile. The celebration we'd had for them was a way to ensure that all the people who supported us over the years had been properly thanked.

On Graduation Day, I dropped Brad off at the campus early, because the graduates had to be at the school two hours before the ceremony. Then I went back home to dress up and get ready for the proceedings.

I wanted to wear a hat to display my pride on this special day, and I had the perfect one in mind. I searched my closet and retrieved my fuchsia straw hat, just the accessory for such a momentous occasion. Then my daughter, my mother, Charles, and I piled into our car.

We found a parking space near the football field, where the ceremony was to take place. The stage was positioned in the middle of the field, and the risers were decorated with red, black, and gold balloons.

We left my mother and Brittany at the bleachers, and Charles and I went searching for closer seats. Making our way through the crowd, we spotted Ms. Perry with her son and beckoned them to sit with us.

Once we were all seated, I scanned the long line of graduates and spotted Brad in his cap and gown. He wore a gold rope to indicate his high grade-point average. His graduation sash was draped across the front of his gown, and he looked just perfect.

Hoping to get his attention, we all waved with excitement and called his name repeatedly, as if he were a rock star. The pride on his face when he saw us really showed, as if he were saying, "Look, we made it!"

Seeing my son in line out there with all the other students, his diploma in one hand and calmly waving to us with the other, I couldn't help myself and started to cry.

After the ceremony, I watched his classmates clamor to take pictures with him, and he smiled for each photo. I remembered how, not so long ago, he'd had to learn how to smile. I realized how much both he and his classmates had grown.

Seeing Brad graduate—with a high school diploma, his friends, and his smile—was a very special and tender moment for me. What an incredible day it was! I was immensely pleased, knowing that we had all done our best to make this triumphant day happen and it did.

Even though it seemed like that day would never come, there we were, reaping the rewards of seeds planted so long before!

Finally Feeling "Normal"

THE TITLE OF THIS CHAPTER says it all: I'm finally feeling "normal." Now that we are well on the other side of high school, and I sit reflecting on all the battles, the phone calls, the letters, and the other advocating tasks, I can breathe a sigh of relief, knowing in my heart that it was all worth it.

As I write this, my son is twenty-five, with more experiences under his belt than many other young men his age. He's going to college and is on target socially.

My dream for Brad is to live fully, gain financial independence, and meet the love of his life, and he has come a long way. He has learned how to comb his hair, brush his teeth, smile, laugh, and look people in the eye when talking to them. He has developed coping skills, such as knowing to stop and get up and walk if he begins rocking incessantly, a nervous tic typical of some people with autism. He has extended his vocabulary tremendously, although he still searches for the right words sometimes...as do many "normal" young people.

I feel sure that his participation in behavioral as well as social programs, such as tap dancing and acting classes, the Boy Scouts, speech contests, taekwondo, and running track, has helped Brad to improve his behavior and definitely contributed to his growth.

The program that I believe was the turning point in his marked improvement was actually the gymnastics class for children with autism. He participated in that class for more than two years, and that was where he demonstrated the greatest strides in improving his coordination.

Brad is now fearless. He personally calls all the people that he has phone numbers for on their birthdays. He has remembered all their birthdates from the moment he first learned of them, and he is a "close friend" that way.

Brad self-selects his foods. When he was in grammar school, one of his classmates asked if he was a vegetarian, probably because he would not eat sandwiches. At that time a typical lunch for him was apples, applesauce, and apple juice. Even now, he never eats lettuce, toast, anything with a granular texture, or most rice (although he will eat shrimp fried rice). Lunch now consists of carrots, three pieces of fruit, and a piece of meat, although still no toast or salads.

Brad likes to wear black, which for him is something akin to a uniform. He is still learning how to gauge the weather or when to wear a jacket.

At home Brad has the job of answering the family phone, which gives him a chance to practice his speech and remembering and relaying messages. As part of his chores, he takes the dog for a walk, vacuums the carpet, washes the dishes, and does his own laundry. Recently, I showed him how to pump gas for us.

Brad can now remember three or four tasks at a time and in which order to do them. When he was eight he was only able to remember one thing at a time, so this is a real accomplishment.

He enjoys doing outside activities, but after spending three or four hours out of the house, he is ready to come home. He then goes to his room to lie down to get some rest, and enjoy some quiet time.

When Brad was in the fourth grade he wanted us to build a two-story house. He was insistent and would talk about it daily. We solved that by buying a model house for him to build. He doesn't talk about that anymore, but his dream is to have his own two-story house one day. Now, I have no doubt that he will.

I remember the times when he would cry when getting his hair cut. This lasted until the age of twelve. We later learned that if the barber started from the back of his head he would not cry. He hasn't cried about that in years. He not only pays for his own haircut but has even learned how to give a tip. (He has been known to give ten dollar tips, however, so I do monitor that.)

I have lived with one foot in the autistic world and one foot in the normal world. It has definitely been a roller coaster ride, but in our household we have learned how to laugh. I also learned a long time ago that preserving my pride was not worth sacrificing my son's growth. The balancing act is knowing when to push for the "normal" experience and when to ask for help.

A lot has changed since Brad was a young boy, and we have worked tirelessly to give him the needed skills to enjoy a full life.

My message is this: There is always hope, so whatever your child's level of ability or disability, just know that things will get better with time, and believe that they will prevail.

I hope my experiences will be helpful to you in working with a family member, student, client or friend with special needs.

Remember: persistence, persistence, persistence!

Finally feeling normal!
Florence Bracy

Family Reflections

Each family member is important to the binding together and thriving of the family unit. Here I have added some reflections from my husband, Charles, and my daughter, Brittany, on their experiences of having a son and brother with special needs.

A Dad's Perspective

I was forty-seven when Brad was born. When you have a long-awaited son, you may have visions of him playing professional sports, for instance, as you yourself dreamed of doing. Baseball and track were my sports in high school, and I remember when he was a toddler I bought a tee-ball set and watched him hit the ball. I was preparing him early for this dream of mine.

When he was six I signed him up for Little League at our local park. I was excited to go out and purchase all the equipment he needed for his burgeoning Little League career. He was on the Mariners team, and he looked great dressed in his purple and gray uniform. Brad had a good throwing arm, was good at running to the bases, and could catch fly balls, but he was having trouble understanding the concept of the game.

When I first realized there might be a problem, he was about seven years old, and we were standing in line for a baseball event we were attending. There was a younger boy about four years old pushing Brad around, and Brad was not defending himself. This was cause for concern.

When he was ten, another incident aroused my concern. A group of boys who lived down the street from our house invited Brad to a sleepover. They often played basketball with Brad in their backyard, so I allowed him to go over for the early evening activities, but not to spend the night. Shortly after going to play, Brad came home crying. I asked him what had happened.

He said, "The boys jumped on me."

I went to talk to Larry, the dad who was hosting the party. He apologized and said that he did not know that had happened. One of the boys then told me that another boy, a twelve-year-old named Michael, had taken a dare to beat up Brad. I explained to the boys that Brad had autism and what they had done wasn't nice, but it was years before Brad went down there again to play.

As Brad got older and taller, the boys down the street began showing him more respect. In fact, Michael, the boy who had jumped on him years ago, comes over to talk to Brad when he's in town visiting his parents, who still live on our street.

For the most part Brad played alone, so I enrolled him in wood carving classes, where they made items like model planes and bird cages. He liked to play basketball in the backyard alone, but he was also in the Boy Scouts in elementary school, and we went on many camping trips with the group.

When he was in middle school I enrolled him in basketball at the local community park. He was still a little uncoordinated; when he was thrown the ball and caught it, he looked like a deer frozen in headlights. He was always a second or two late in responding to the plays. His saving grace was that he could shoot a ball with accuracy from a very long range. When he was thrown the ball to make a shot, the crowd would yell, "Shoot, Brad, shoot!" I would sit there beaming with pride, hearing the crowd call my son's name. Ultimately, his downfall was his inability to remember the plays the coach had created for the team.

I took it upon myself to go to a resource fair at the Regional Center, my first experience entering the world of the developmentally disabled. I saw many adults and young people there with greater physical and mental challenges than Brad.

When I returned home, my wife asked me how the experience was. I told her, "Things could be worse. I am happy with the hand we were dealt with."

At my first autism conference, I attended a workshop for fathers of children with autism. The workshop made me feel more connected to that world, and it was interesting to hear the various fathers' points of view.

I took a clear message away from that group, that it would be a challenge to give our children the support they need. Autism has no conscience, and it doesn't care if you're rich or poor or what your ethnicity may be. It's a reality and a challenge that families need to accept without feeling ashamed.

Brad and I often have discussions, when we talk about anything he doesn't understand. He and I attend two different churches of his choice together. We alternate each month. I drive him to whatever event he wants to attend, such as the theater, dancing, or sporting events, because driving is a challenge for him.

Like every other young man his age, he gets a little bull-headed at times, and we have to go eye to eye and man to man and have "manly" talks. I try to explain to him that I have a little more experience than he does and can help him avoid making mistakes that he will later regret. Some of the general fatherly advice I have given him includes such ideas as these: Don't smoke or drink, never run from the police, never steal anything, and don't let people push you or try to hurt you in any way.

My son's graduation ranked among the proudest days of my life—to see that, regardless of the challenges he had faced, he was able to graduate with his peers. He dressed well, spoke well, and made me prouder than I ever thought possible. It was a moment in our lives that I will always treasure.

My hopes for him are that he continues to be a strong, lovable son and continues his quest to learn as much as possible. I am optimistic about him finding a mate who understands him and is willing to work along with him. I also hope that he finds a job that is a good match for him and one which he enjoys. Challenges, certainly—there are still a lot of things ahead that he may not yet understand, such as accepting responsibility on a job or understanding how the system works in terms of housing, transportation, and medical care.

I didn't have a relationship with my own father. He lived in another state, so I never felt a strong bond with him. When he died I promised myself that I would be a better father to my two children than my father was to me. I tried to set a good example by taking care of my family responsibly and being there for them. I promised myself that I would always be there to support both my children. Despite the difficulties of raising a special needs son, it never crossed my mind to give up, because Brad is my loved one.

My advice for fathers of children with a disability is, strive to do your best to be strong and supportive. There is nothing to be ashamed of. Don't be disappointed if they can't do all the things you expect of them, and remember always to love them for who they are. As for the difficulties, you will learn to talk about them and find solutions.

Too many fathers abandon their children when they have autism or some other disability and leave the mothers to bear all of the responsibilities. My advice to fathers is to be thankful for your son or daughter with autism. All you have to do is love them and be supportive.

God didn't put you here by yourself. There are other families struggling with similar conditions. Autism requires us all to work together in order to better understand and help and support our kids.

> *My daughter, Brittany, was fifteen when her brother was diagnosed at the age of eight. At the beginning of this book I revealed part of a conversation I had with my daughter after letting her read my journal. I then turned the tables and asked her how she felt about her brother and his diagnosis. These were her answers, in her own words.*

A Sister's Perspective

So, I am asking you, how did you feel about your brother?

I knew he was different in some ways, but I didn't really know until I was volunteering at the camp and saw that he acted different than the other kids at the camp. I was comparing his behavior to them, and I could see a difference. Once a diagnosis was made, and he was getting additional help, I just accepted that this is how he behaves.

How did Brad's diagnosis affect your relationship with him?
It definitely stifled our relationship. Between feeling embarrassed about his behavior and not being able to communicate with him fully, I distanced myself from him. Even now, our relationship can only go to a certain point because of where he is developmentally. I would love to have a "normal" sibling relationship. I wish it was possible, but because of his autism, we will never be able to have that growing, mature sister/brother relationship.

Did you feel there was less attention paid to you by your parents due to Brad's needs?
Not at all. Our age gap definitely helped that. We were in such different phases developmentally that we had different things going on and different needs.

But how did you feel about his disability?
I was embarrassed! When he would repeat lines from movies or would stare off in space like he didn't understand what I was saying to him, I felt embarrassed. I remember when he was a teenager, my then boyfriend and I were trying to teach Brad how to talk to girls and how to look at a girl without staring nervously. That was funny. Now he knows how to sneak a peek at girls in passing

without staring strangely, and he can go up to someone and have a cordial conversation.

What was the social impact for you as a young woman, having a family member with special needs?
Initially, I was embarrassed by his behavior when my friends would come by. I couldn't explain why he was so socially awkward, and I didn't understand why he was so different.

What is the one piece of advice you would give to other families who have children with special needs?
Be as supportive as you can towards your family, and try to put yourself in the shoes of the family member with autism.

What was your experience on Brad's Graduation Day?
I was incredibly proud of him. I observed all the hard work he put forth to get to graduation, as well as the constant collaboration our mother and dad were involved in to make sure Brad received what he needed. The day was almost surreal!

Final Words

Recently, someone asked me about my career and how Brad's diagnosis affected it. Here's what I had to say.

Most of my jobs gave me the flexibility to make the phone calls and write the letters to get the services Brad needed. I knew that I could not take a job that required a lot of travel, because he needed me to help with homework and take him to his therapies, such as speech, vision, gymnastics, and social programs.

I would not have done it any other way. I put in the time it took to take care of my son, and it paid off. This has been my career as a mom, to ensure that my children have the best life and can navigate their way through it, to the best of their ability. I am eternally grateful for the partnership that Charles and I have in raising our son. His commitment to our family and to Brad is unquestioned.

I hope the story of our journey is helpful to you in supporting your child, family member, or community member with special needs.

With great pride, I would like to acknowledge my son, Brad, for typing from my handwritten journal the first draft of the manuscript of this book so that all can read our story.

Florence Bracy

Resources

Autism

Autism Society

www.autism-society.org

Signs of Autism

www.cdc.gov/ncbddd/autsim/freematerial.html

Autism Speaks

www.autismspeak.org

CDC-Center for Disease Control

www.cdc.gov/ncbddd/autsim/freematerial.html

National Society for Autism

www.nationalautismassociation.org

Education

Carousel School

www.carouselschool.com

Special education for autism, asperger's, and down syndrome

Early childhood education (LAUSD)

www.lausd.net/sped

Special Education services for Los Angeles Unified School District

Kayne Eras Center

www.ect.net/school

Special education school servicing ages 5-22

Marlton School for the Deaf

www.marltonschool.org

Provides services for ages Pre K-22, school for the deaf and hard of hearing

Pathways UCLA Extension

www.uclaextenstion.edu/pathway

Education program for young adults with intellectual disabilities: the students live on the campus and learn independent living skills

The HELP Group

www.thehelpgroup.org

Provides support for seven non-public schools, counseling for children and their families

The Frostig Center

www.frostig.org

Provides support for learning differences

The Jeffrey Foundation

www.thejeffreyfoundation.com

Provides recreation educational and social programs for special needs children

Total Education Solutions

www.tesidea.com

Provides specialized services to children and adults with exceptional needs

Westmark School

www.westmarkschool.org

Provides students with language based learning differences and an exceptional college-preparatory environment

Employment

Ability First Employment Program

www.abilityfirst.org

Provides programs for special needs adults and children

Giant Steps Training Program

www.giantsteps.net

Work training program for adults

OPARC

www.oparc.org

Provides adult daycare services and vocational programs

Peak Performance

www.pptcenters.com

Adult day care, training and vocational program

Social Vocational Services

www.socialvocationalservices.org

Day programs, work and vocational programs

Wiley Center

www.wileycenter.org

Provides comprehensive treatment and vocational programs for adults with autism

Government

Access Services

www.accessla.org

Provides transportation to persons with disabilities

CA Departure of Developmental Services

www.dds.ca.gov

Provides services to support individuals with developmental disabilities

California Department of Rehabilitation

www.dor.ca.gov

Provides employment and resources for individuals who are disabled

Regional Centers

www.dds.ca.gov/RC/RClist.cfm

Social Security

www.ssa.gov

Health and Medical

Behavior

Behavior Tech
www.behaviortech.net

Behavior Therapy Clinic
www.behaviortherapyclinic.com

Dental

USC Herman Ostrow School of Dentistry
www.dentistry.usc.edu

Loma Linda University School of Dentistry
www.llu.edu/koppel-center/dentalservices

Digestive Problems

Digestive Disorders
www.csacellacs.org

Other Health-related Organizations

National Association for Mental Illness
www.nami.org
Organization that provides support for families who have family members that have mental illness

Reach Across LA

www.reachacrossla.org

Programs and therapies for mental health and dual diagnosis

Recording for Blind and Dyslexic

www.rfbd.org

Provides support for the blind and dyslexic

Hospitals

Children's Hospital of Los Angeles

www.chla.org

Huntington Children's Medical Center

www.huntingtonhosptial.org

Orange County Children's Medical Center

www.choc.org/child's_healthchoc_difference

Southern California Orthopedic Institute

www.bone-joint-muscle-nerve.org

Language treatment, bone, joint, muscle in children and adults

Stanford Medical Center

www.med.standford.edu/autismcenter.html.

Provides autism assessments, treatments and research

Stramski Children's Developmental Center

Miller Children's Hospital in Long Beach

www.millerchildshospitallb.org/

Comprehensive care from birth-21; behavior and developmental conditions; autism, ADHD/ADD, down syndrome, and learning disabilities

University of San Francisco Medical Center

www.ucsfbenioffchildrens.org/clinics.edu

Provides assessments, therapy and research for autism

UCLA Center for Autism Research and Treatment (CART)

www.semel.ucla.edu/autism/research

Provides assessments, therapy and research for autism

UCLA Peers Clinic

www.semel.ucla.edu/peers

Social skills training for adolescent and adults

Housing

Ability First

www.abilityfirst.org

Provides affordable and accessible housing for the developmental disabled

Devereaux

www.devereaux.org

Adult residential facility for developmental delayed

Five Acres

www.5acres.org/programs

Residential facility and programs

Hathway-Sycamore Child and Family Services

www.hathaway-sycamore.org

Residential facility and programs

Hillside Home for Children

www.hillsidesorg/programs/residential-treatment-services

Residential facility and program

Optimist For Boys

www.oyhfs.org

Residential facility for boys

LA County Section 8

www.socialsesrvice.com/tenant/

Provides housing for low income and disabled

Legal and Advocacy

Elissa Henkin

www.elissahenkin.com

Special Ed advocate for pre-k through adult

Disability Rights

www.disablityrightsca.org

Protects rights of individuals with disabilities

Law Offices of Arlene Bell

www.arlenebell.com

Advocates and represents children with special needs

Learning Rights Law Center

www.learningrights.org

Legal rights nonprofit represents children with special needs

Martin & Martin LLP

www.martin-martin.net

Firm specializes in special education, civil rights and employment discrimination

Newman, Aaronson Vanaman

www.havlaw.net

Represents children with disabilities needing specialized legal services

Public Counsel

www.publiccounsel.org

Provides support to individuals with special needs

Special Needs Network

www.snn.org

Provides parent advocacy training, conferences and workshops

Occupational and Physical Therapy

Therapy West

www.therapywest.org

Provides occupational therapy

Pediatric Therapy

www.pediatrictherapynetwork.org

Provides occupational and speech therapy

Every Child Achieves

www.everychildachieves.com

Provides occupational therapy

Napa Center

www.napacenter.org

Provides occupational, physical and speech therapy

Speech

Briggs Associates

www.briggsandassociates.com

Provides speech therapy

Children's Speech Care Center

www.childspeech.net

Provides speech therapy for children

L.A. Speech and Language Therapy Center

www.speakla.com

Provides assessments and therapy for speech for ages 3-adult and other comprehensive services for those with autism

Linda Mood Bell

www.lindamoodbell.com

Language and literary processing instruction

Listening and Spoken Language Knowledge Center

ww.agbell.org

Sports and Recreation

Aceing Autism
www.utsa.com/Adult-Tennis/aceing_autism.programs_expands_across_country
Tennis for child and adults with autism

AYSO VIP Soccer
www.ayso.org
Soccer for children and adults with disabilities

Best Buddies
www.bestbuddies.org
Provides opportunities for socialization and employment

All-Abilities Dance
www.allabilitiesdance.org
Dance and drama program for disabled youth

Born to Act
www.borntoactplayers.com
Performing arts, voice, dance and drama

Broadway Gymnastics School
www.broadwaygym.com/specialed.php

LA Jets Track Club
www.lajetstrackclub.org
Running club for all children

Mychal's Place

www.mychal's.org

Recreation and employment training center for disabled children and youth

Performing Art Studio West

www.pstudiowest.com

Training developmental disabled, working in film, television and commercials

Queue-Up

www.queue-up.org

Therapeutic horseback riding

Special Olympics

www.specialolympic.org

Offers a variety of competitive sports for the disabled

UCLA Recreation

www.recreation.ucla.edu/adaptive programs

Provides activities for special needs individuals

Support Groups

Fiesta Educativa

www.fiestaeducation.org

Dedicated to empowering familes of persons with disabilities

HAAF

www.haafii.org

Parent support group for parents of children with autism

Korean American Special Education Center

www.kasecca.org

Promotes understanding of developmental and mental disabilities

TACA

www.taca.org

Parent support and advocacy group

Vista Del Mar & Child & Family Services

www.vistadelmar.org

Support group for parents and individuals with aspergers

Resources Outside of California

Autism Society of America

www.autism-society.org

National Autism Association

www.nationalautismassociation.org

Autism Speaks

www.autismspeaks.org

International Listings of Autism Organizations

International Autism Organizations

www.autism.org.uk/services/helplines/outside-uk/round-world.aspx

*Disclaimer:

I have made an effort to provide a comprehensive list of resources to get readers started on their own journey. By no means is it a complete list of all the services available. The inclusion of any organization or agency does not imply or constitute an endorsement, nor does exclusion or omission imply disapproval.

HELPFUL HINTS

HERE ARE A FEW TIDBITS of advice to help you in supporting your special needs child.

1. **Listen to your child.** There might be something that they're interested in that you can give them exposure to; an instrument, hobby, sports, skills, book etc. something that you might also be interested in as well.
2. **Call their name.** When giving directions or speaking to them, call their name first to get their attention so they know you are talking to them.
3. **Appreciate the things that your special needs child can do.** Get them involved in family activities such as answering the phone, leading family discussions or prayer, making grocery lists, taking the trash out, cleaning out a drawer or closet.
4. **Praise them in front of family members for work well done.** This is important so family members acknowledge that the special needs child has value. Incorporate them into the daily activities of your home. Don't assume that

because they have special needs, they are incapable of being a vital part of the family.

5. **Make sure both of you are well hydrated and well rested and have eaten recently.** All of this can help in maintaining your patience with them and with their behavior.
6. **Collaborate with parents, organizations, and agencies.** Meet with other parents or neighbors to work in partnership to accomplish goals for your child. Put teams together for your special needs child in the areas of medical care, education, and social issues.
7. **Advocate for your child** if there are any opportunities for club memberships, church activities, or leadership positions for which your special needs child has a talent.
8. **Have specific goals for your special needs child**. These can be put into a plan. For instance, you might set goals every six months in the areas of Family, Fun, Faith, Fitness, and Future.
9. **Special needs children also need to have great expectations for their lives.** The celebrations and activities may look different from traditional forums or formats, but they are still being celebrated.
10. **Have Faith**. Faith does work, and miracles do happen when you expect them!

ABOUT THE AUTHOR

FLORENCE BRACY WAS BORN IN Los Angeles and grew up in Pasadena, California.

Ms. Bracy facilitates support groups for parents and caregivers of people with autism. In addition, she is a special needs advocate, representing children with special needs at administrative hearings.

She was recognized by the state of California for her work in the special needs community and was selected to serve on the Interagency Coordinating Council for Early Intervention. This board serves as an advisory council on policy for the state Department of Developmental Services.

Her education includes studying at Pacific University in Forest Grove, Oregon, California State University, Los Angeles, and UCLA. She earned her BA in Speech Communications and is certified in Public Relations, Special Needs Advocacy, and Paralegal Studies.

She lives in Los Angeles with her husband of thirty years, Charles, and their son, Brad. Their daughter, Brittany, is married and has two children. Florence enjoys reading, walking in charity fundraisers, writing, cooking, and she especially enjoys spending time with her family.

This is her first published book.

Florence Bracy is available for speaking engagements, workshops, conferences, and other special events. To inquire, please visit www.florencebracy.com

Florence Bracy's social media information is as follows:

Facebook: Florence Bracy

Made in the USA
Columbia, SC
28 February 2018